GET
FRESH BOOKS

Praise for

## THE LITTLE DEATHS

From searing to sweet, Mercy's poems pull us into a maelstrom of passion, cynicism, ecstasy, fury, and joy so that we may understand the fullness of womanhood. Her words illuminate the often perilous path that black women have to walk to simply find the space to say, I am.

—Keisha-Gaye Anderson, author of
*A Spell for Living, Everything Is Necessary,* and *Gathering the Waters*

Mercy Tullis-Bukhari's work is a portrait that's been painted over multiple times, beautiful in each layer. Her words are fearless, vulnerable, strong, confessional, erotic, historical & wonderfully personal. Whether it's about The Atlantic, or Arawaks, Co-Op  or The Grand Concourse, *The Little Deaths*, will have you coming back looking for all the secrets & colors she has in these poems.

—Bonafide Rojas, author of
*Notes on the Return to the Island, When the City Sleeps,* and
*Pelo Bueno: A Day in the Life of a Nuyorican Poet*

Mercy Tullis-Bukhari's poetics glides from social justice to erotica to women empowerment, all the while elevating Black narratives and challenging the fragility of the American dream.

—Ron Kavanaugh, publisher of
*Mosaic;* executive director of *Literary Freedom Project: One Book One Bronx*

# THE LITTLE DEATHS

poems

Mercy Tullis-Bukhari

**Get Fresh Publishing, A Non-Profit Corp.**
PO Box 901,
Union, NJ 07083

www.gfbpublishing.org

Library of Congress Control Number: 2023932860

ISBN 9798218148539

Cover, layout, typesetting, and design:
**culture glut llc**
cultureglut.com

This book was typeset in Bembo.

*For Marvin*

# Table of Contents

## La Gringa's First Ride to Los Hondos

Esta Gringa flew to Honduras when she was five years old on
the lie that she was going to meet Mickey Mouse because
esta Gringa could not stop crying while boarding this
monstrous-size thing that was supposed to stay afloat

high in the air. We flew from Kennedy Airport into
clouds, then over pineapple plantations & banana fields, cows
roaming & campesinos working, sand & beaches con
hondos *strong as the ancestors pleading from esta grown Gringa*

*to go back.* Once grounded, esta Gringa asked, Bueno,
Where is Mickey Mouse? Because, of course, Mickey Mouse should
be waiting for esta Gringa on the tarmac. Her mami ignored the
question, pushed esta Gringa pass the initial slap of hot humid air,
took her down the aircraft stairs, walked her across the tarmac
into the building of the airport. We searched for our suitcases
in a room where suitcases were thrown at random places on
the floor. We were like roaches scattering when the light goes

on, looking for our bags, yelling across the room "encontre una"
when we found each bag. Mami, slipping a ten US to the woman
who patted the top of the tightly packed suitcases—clothes & soaps
& shoes & more clothes & ducktaped packages from Tia
Melba y Tia Lorna y Tia Carmen (not really mis tias), for abuelita,
fulano y fulano y fulano. We returned to the airport the

following week for one missing suitcase. Esta Gringa, played
futbolito barefooted in the sand that was her soil. In the confused
gaze of neighbors, esta Gringa swam in granules, & poured
buckets on her head. Esta Gringa washed it off her body in the
big sink behind the house, the same sink Mami used to handwash
our clothes. Esta Gringa chased chickens, danced punta, ate

la comida of split coconuts, heard her Mami yell to curious
passerbys con urgullo, "¡Ella es Gringa! ¡Ciudana Americana!"
*Esta grown Gringa looks back at a time when Gringa status*

*mattered.* She watched a Garifuna man walk to a canoe with a net,
come back to shore with fish in his net. She watched a Garifuna
woman take a fish from that net, scrape the scales of that fish, split
it open, salt & fried the fish en aceite de coco. Mami squeezed lime
on the fried fish & tajadas. Esta Gringa, ate fried fish con tajadas

for lunch every day. Gracias a dios, Columbus said, that Honduras saved
his lost ass from the depths of the storm, y esta Gringa was

saved from a contrived fantasy world of fake-believe dreams
and its minstrel mouse.

# Dinner with a Jinn

I saw a jinn at my door so I invited him in
& told him *have a seat.* I told him
*I lost my wallet, amongst*

*other important stuff* & I told him
*give me my shit back,* he said no.
I said, *would you like dinner, then?*

*I make a mean lasagna.* He said,
he had heard about my lasagna, &
that he was going to stay to eat. He said,

he was going to keep taking from me,
while I made lasagna for him. He said,
he was going to take whatever he wanted.

I said, *c'mon, be nice to me.* He said,
go make that lasagna. He took my laptop,
my favorite pen, my phone & my car keys.

He sat on my couch with his hand
in his pants drinking a beer,
burping loudly, while watching black

women fighting on a show about hip
hop or basketball or something. *The
lasagna is ready* I told him. He told

me that mountains will open and
clowns will come out to sprinkle
glitter on my doubts. He ate my

lasagna, from the pan. I said,
*give me my shit back.* He said no,
told me my lasagna was not all that.

The jinn put all he stole atop my favorite blanket,
gathered the corners of the blanket together,
swung the package over his shoulder & then, disappeared.

## Loose Change

I don't understand throwing coins in fountains,
throwing, what one would call, loose change,
then making a wish. I see pennies, nickels,
dimes, & even quarters. I guess the value of the coin
coincides with the desperation of the wish
to be made real. I remember when we used to search
for loose change—change that may have fallen out
of pockets—in couches, just to have dinner.
I want to put my hand in the chemically treated water
& put their dreams in my pockets. Our wish was to find
enough change to pour on the supermarket counter
& buy a slim pack of meat for dinner on a given night.

## 1940 University Avenue, Holy Spirit School Gym,
## The Bronx

It was a small school, Holy Spirit, with only one class per grade.
Our principal, Mrs. McEvoy, was a tall, broad, hefty Irish-Bronx

woman with a curly red 'fro. Every morning in the gym, before
marching to our classrooms, we initiated our day with prayer &

pledge in our school gym. Each grade/class lined up in two lines
with boys on the left & girls on the right. Grades 1–4 were set

up on the right side of the gym & grades 5–8 on the left side.
"HSS" was painted in the middle of the varnished floor of the gym.

Mrs. McEvoy, holding a brown bead rosary, a huge cross
everyone in the gym could see, & a brass bell that always reflected

the gym lights shine, stood in the middle of the gym. She was still,
stoic, facing the door as we lined up in our designated places.

We lined up like soldiers waiting for instructions.
Once we were in our lines, she rang her bell, & we quietly waited

for her to greet us with *Good Morning, Holy Spirit Students.* We
always responded with *Good morning, Mrs. McEvoy.* The whole

school, grades 1–8, said good morning to Mrs. McEvoy, in sing-song.
We started with the rosary, reciting ten *Hail Marys* as Mrs. McEvoy's

fingers went from one bead to the next, then concluded our prayer with
One *Our Father.* After we honored Mary, Jesus, & God, in that order,

we ended our morning assembly—right hand on our chest to pledge
allegiance to our flag, then sang praises to our country. We were dismissed

from morning assembly, grade by grade, as Mrs. McEvoy
called the grades, we marched to our classrooms:

divorces, abortions, & infidelities—I yearn for an era of lines,
consistency, & order. I knew my line, under a rosary, a brass bell,
& Mrs. McEvoy. I now spend my life finding lines under nothing.

# Braiding Kadeem's Hair

*Can you braid the sides?*

Kadeem asked me to braid his hair. He just graduated
from college & will be going on interviews soon.

I wanted to tell him that he will not get a job with braided hair.

My boy would have been Kadeem's age—
I was 16 when I ended the fetus. Three chunks of hair
weaved into each other into a braid—
into the ghost of my emptied womb.

I closed my eyes while braiding, giving flesh to the ghost
placed on the chair in front of me.

*You will not get a job with braided hair, my love,*
I say in my heart.

Kadeem thanks me while I am braiding, & the flesh
becomes a ghost again. I feel the sting in my belly
when Kadeem speaks.

I keep braiding because my child never—

**erupt contain**

here you go, the sun the moon the stars &
everything in between, take my hand, tell me
your fears your goals your dreams, let me feed
you fried chicken & burritos & my hard length &
feigned futures while i slip my hand between your
deafening thighs, watch the ghosts of the little deaths
dance around you, laughing at your expectations, drip
into my fingers, after i make you come to the womanhood
you so desperately suppressed, lick my fingers, kiss me,
again, again, again, but just so that you understand, just so
that you also take this in—i must go back to her

my touch—your eyes, make me want you more, your breath
in my mouth, your taste in my life, my hand on your heart,
my lips on you, i feel your heart murmur, feel your heart remember
a rhythm, i trample on the trails other men burrowed for me, drop
burnt rose petals on the paths to the cloaked corners inside of you
don't cry, don't cry, don't cry, my pretty little whore—
my what-she-does-not-give-me, don't cry, just turn around &
bend over, because you already know, i will go back to her

you know, you know, you already know, these things never end well

look at me, look at me, watch me go to her, look at the green fairy dancing
with the ghosts of your little deaths, let green dust from my absinthe eyes
float you to sleep

## Gray Pubic Hair

you crept out of nowhere, bitch
you decide to appear

there

i see you
reminding me
of the little deaths
i barely have, dried
by the big one
soon to come

## First Mammogram

I am in the waiting room
wearing my pink hospital
gown, waiting to be called.
I watch shows about healthy
options, about food swaps
& demos of low-impact exercises.
I can take 1/3 of the pasta from
a mac 'n cheese recipe, &
use cauliflower instead.
For chocolate chip cookies, I
can use half white flour
& half whole wheat flour
instead of all white flour. I must move
daily, according to the television,
& do my estate planning & will.
A woman without hair walks
into the waiting room. I am
not going to assume that her
visit is a follow-up, simply
because of where we are
& her being bald. I am going
to start my estate planning
& add whole wheat flour
to my shopping list.

# On Aging

I just want to stay hot enough
for a 25-year-old to masturbate
                to me.

## Velvet Poster, 1981

Claws grip her neck, a skull draped
over her earth, her stare pulls
my hand to the smoothness of her skin.
Brown flesh, afro, & breasts protrude
from the poster in velvet. I feel the engraved
curve of a woman—jungle vines backdrop
my pre-teen imagination, their thickness &
hair-like texture, swirl like my pre-pubic hair.

## Calgon

Calgon, where the fuck are you?

Well, then—

all I can do is keep my scratched-up
Ray Bans crispy, & walk on—

**Illegalities**

I am usually the driver,
but he is so caught up in male ego
that even though we are both drunk,

he insists that he drives. I look up
through the sunroof & see the clouds
floating still while we are moving,

my bare feet hanging out the window,
my senses swimming in fermentation.
My toes open & close, let the air through.

I see a little girl, too young, legally, to sit
in the front seat of a car, asleep, her head
on her elbow, sticking out of the window.

But we are drunk, I tell myself, before judgement
creeps in. Bicycle riders pass us,
the light turns green, we move forward.

Slow down muthafucker, a bike rider yells at us.
But we are slow, the bike rider just isn't paying
attention. We are blasting Afrobeat from our car, &

drivers peek in. They look away when I look back at them.
I offer him a blowjob while he is driving.
He says, *Not yet.*

## The Heeled Journey

At the age of nine I started out with tiny heels, high enough
to keep me off the ground, thin enough for me to practice my walk,
a sway that confused grown men. I practiced my posture & walk
with the focus of a child learning to ride a bike without training wheels.

I learned the balance of womanhood with a Britannica on my head.
The hallway of our apartment— the runway for Latina womanhood,
while my mother directed & my father watched approvingly.

*Una mujer tiene que saber cómo caminar en tacones,* my mother said.
What became playtime—putting on my mother's lipstick, sliding my
feet into her high-heeled shoes, wearing her dresses & hats

as costumes—the definite definition of my gender. In those
mini stilts, I was still a determined nine-year old girl. Those shoes
compressed my toes but did not suppress my tag & double-dutch.

Over time, the heels grew higher & thinner. Compliments on how
well I walked, how much height I'd gained, filled the empty rooms
inside of me. But when I became a woman, truly became a woman,

my body no longer wanted tacones. My feet absorbed life's shots
over years that weakened my knees & strained my back. I kept
the tacones in boxes & knew, for me to walk further I needed

my feet to be closer to the ground. When I hear my mother say
*Pero, ya no eres mujer,* I pull out shoes she would approve of
for evenings out & family parties. *Póntelo,* my mother says.

After hours in tacones, I peel them off my swollen feet,
& spread my toes to release the tension. I massage my feet
with Vaseline, & elevate my legs on deep, feathered pillows.

My daughter watches me reset my foundation. I see her, accepting —
the time has come for her to be trained.

## Apology to My Ancestors

for allowing the hypersexuality of the white gaze to smother my ancient beliefs,
        my role as the sacred feminine the alpha of this universe
                for criticizing my black & brown kin as we live our lives in the —
                        for my idleness against the imbalance of power
                                for thinking that suppressing my greatness —

for not walking the path you died making for me
        for not knowing my imagination is the freedom that carries me forward
        for not seeing that my spirit is the soil you were stolen from & the new —
                for not valuing my role as a mother because for so many of you, —
                        for allowing the disjointing of my family and our —
                                for allowing the outside to infect my hopes —
                                        for all those times I silenced your —
                                                for not living the life you —

I am sorry        for        even the slight question of
        my skin
                my nose
                        my hair
                                my lips

I confess
I have spent too much
of my life insulting you,
when knew who you were, who you wanted me to be.

Your spirits haunt the Atlantic, your souls the Americas

I am sorry                my spirits                my ancestors

— mental plantations of our injustices, blocked from seeing our beauty,

— would uplift others


— world you built
— that role was stolen
— communities
— with their venom
— voices, keeping me from being my true self
— wanted for me

for creating the chains          you never allowed

# I Was My America, Cristóbal Colón

I am the 9-year old girl,
Who was sold to be pimped.

I was free, free to roam my land
Without the threat of your forcing me
Into Christian Barbarity—
I played, in the lands of my ancestors and
Called to clouds and leaves for guidance
I am now a whore
Forced to be chained, unclothed
To be sold,
to Christian men

Who is this God you speak of?
This god who tells them
that my pain is their redemption?
That My Innocence should be blackened
by their whiteness?
That my virginity must be their blood
dripping from the thorns of that crown?
That crown that adorns a man who
does not resemble my king?

I am a 13-year old boy,
Who can no longer cry.
I carry my hands where
I once carried stones and
jewels. I saw my brother get eaten by their dogs.
I saw my father get burned by their fire.
I saw my mother get fucked by their disease.

I wanted to help them.
I wanted to live.
I wanted to give you the
yellow elements you wanted so desperately.
I wanted to believe under all
the evil you would pardon my existence.

I have no tears.
I eat my food like the dogs you
release into our lands—

Know, that I will see my people on the other side.
And know, that I will meet your God with your cross
Between my teeth.

# Peacock

I am still that child
wearing peacock feathers

I was not supposed to be—
conceived out of purposefully missed birth control pills,
that placed shackles on a man who wanted an out.

Yet, I am not the most consistent myself.
Bonds are as minimal as the everyday,
with no grounding of earth, chance, love.

I still venture into family grounds
To find brothers and sisters who
Lack the native tongue and experiences

and an interest in peacocks.

# Dead Deer on the Hutch

I dress my children in their coats then their gloves then their hats I put Chapstick on their lips while they put their backpacks on their backs the elevator delayed again I hope the payroll secretary excuses my lateness again I drive five miles above the local speed limit angered by the yellow bus stop sign I see the unmarked police car a block away I get to my children's school with kisses I rush them in the building and jump back into my car to get on the Hutch going south.

I see a dead deer.

Not on the Westchester side of the Hutch but on The Bronx side.

On the left shoulder of the highway,
I see its body lying on the edge
with its rump protruding into the
fast lane.  I once saw a dead deer encased in
crystal bubbles, standing upright, staring at me
as I devalued its presence with a photo from my
iPhone. I wished I had a professional camera
to capture the glistening from its crystal bubbles to
memorialize the smile it had while standing dead.

Strike a pose, deer. *I'm most alive in crystal.*

My mother brought deer meat from Arizona once, two weeks
before her heart attack. She died. I threw the deer out because I wanted to live.
My father saw food being wasted.

Deer still roam in The Bronx
behind co-op buildings and the newly built Macy's
by the congested bottleneck exits
through the patch of grain, or whatever those long thingies are

I'm a Bronx girl and I just saw a dead deer on the Hutch.
If those long thingies really were grain, someone would have
capitalized on that land by now, right? Made bread or something.

*Come get your Bronx Bread!*

Maybe it was a dead dog. A really big dog.

In my world of grain and deer in crystal, I want to believe that
I saw a dead deer on the Hutch, on The Bronx side.

# Bronx Wild Turkey Off the Bruckner

A turkey wanders under the Whitestone Multiplex sign
bordering the school buses parked in the abandoned lot
picking through the dried bush of the untrimmed greenery.
In its quest for sustenance on Bronx land, it sees the drive-thru,
and the Algonquin, and my family movie nights on days
my mother and father were almost friendly,
floating under the perpetual for-sale sign.

I am sitting in my car, in traffic, alongside the Whitestone.
The turkey looks at me when I take my smartphone
out of my bag. I take a picture of the turkey. The picture, in silence
mode, still makes a sound and the turkey, after the picture,
moves its beak up to look at me with squinted eyes and
a tilted head. That look was an old school Bronx look. You
gave that look to bitches on the block who were messing
with your man who talked about you behind your back
who you just did not like for reasons you could not explain
but you still gave that look.

The look forces my eyes and camera phone away.
I thought, the turkey is about to attack me or, as we B-X people say,
I'm about to get jumped.

## A Kiss Below A Platform

You walked in the middle of the tracks at the Baychester Avenue train station. The 5 train was parked a station away at Dyre Ave, and you walked on the tracks, I guess to show your 14-year-old bravado. You were in slacks and in a tie. I, in my uniform skirt, not yet rolled up because we were freshmen and I was not yet privy to the tricks of Catholic high school girls, walked on the platform, parallel to you.

You looked at the tracks through active electricity, careful of your steps, fueled by danger, thrilled by my being impressed, to display your erotic excitement for me at an age when we were still sexless. I looked at you from guilty excitement, fascinated the first time a boy went to extremes to impress me. Come back up, I told you.

Like a swimmer getting out of a pool, I was your focal point when you pulled yourself up with your arms. You walked to me, took both of my hands to pull me closer to you. Your look made me smile. I looked away, infused by the tingles I had never felt. You kissed my cheek, then my neck. I looked at you, then you kissed me on my lips. I felt your tongue, delicious and smooth, like a the tamarindo piragüa I had the day before.

When we stopped, you said we looked like a rainbow of brown. You said, "I am caramel and you are milk chocolate. We could melt our sweets in the same pot, make caramel chocolate candies to feed the world with our combined sweetness." I smiled, imagining us feeding the world with Snickers bars. I liked the good stuff, though, the Lindt truffles from the pharmacy. We are going to be better than Lindt chocolates, you and me, I thought.

I saw you with a brown girl that was your brown, who was not from our Bronx. I remembered the way you smiled from the tracks. I remember watching you smile while looking at the tracks, knowing that I was watching every single one of your almost deathly steps. The same smile you had for me, I saw you give her. I still smiled at you, when you were with her. You looked at me, put your head down, held one of her hands, and walked her away.

You said we could feed the world with our sweetness. Being with her, I guess will hold your elevated race in the caste of browns. I'm at the bottom, I know, as a foundation. You looked down, and you no longer saw me. I looked up, and I saw your creating buildings with her. Your walk on the train tracks through jungles of electricity was like the chance you took in losing your place in the caste of browns when you kissed a dark-skinned Black girl.

## Feed

Sometimes, it's not easy to approach feed.
With careful precision, you sit and watch
what you will conquer. You move when it
moves, following closely, seeing, waiting
for an opening of possibly attacking. A bite,
a quick attack when he looks elsewhere. It
could be just a scratch. Just a scratch, the feed
thinks. Then, you watch, following him,
keeping a distance but still vigilant. Your
sweat drops are oozing through your pores.
You watch, blending under bushes and stalks
but he still sees you. You move away, but you
know you have conquered. The end is near
for him, and soon he will collapse within his
last attempt to avoid you. You lower into stalks
with predatory preciseness. With patience and
prayer, you watch the bite engulf his body. At
collapse, you soothe your feed. It was not
personal, you tell him.

## To the Canadian Goose in Co-Op City

I assume your ancestors roamed the land
we made into sewage, then Freedomland,
then built towers with mild materials for the sake of
trapping humans in chambers. We constructed
buildings that are now sinking into the waste.
The webbed feet will keep you above the waste,
and above us when we sink within the chambers
of our towers. It was only one tower in Babel,
though, and all of us will sink in the sewage
below us. My Canadian Goose friend, I will
not be mad if you paddle by my drowning body
as I reach for your wing. I have seen so many of
your brethren, flatten on the highways with
feathers floating above as each car rapes through
their already flattened bodies.

I want webbed feet. I want it all, I say. I want to
walk on land and swim on water. I want to be
called Jesus. My Canadian Goose friend, you are
the Jesus of Co-Op City, and I am just Judas.

## Bitches

I was a girl when you told me
that women were like dogs for you.
You play with them, toss a ball,
then you send them away,
just to watch them come back for more

I was confused, when you tossed
me away, so effortlessly.

I became a woman, when I caught
the ball and swallowed it,
and kept running away—

# Mind Fuck

I arrived wearing tight jeans and stilettos
wanting a love story to end the fucks
that only made me come—
          to a stop sign.
Unlove for self
but lust for a simple wink or a baseless smile
still gave me hope.
Hope—
in a Disney dream of kisses
to wake me from
nightmares of mutha-fuckers darting my soul,
who just really wanted to get a piece of this ass.

I got it.  I knew who I was—

a little girl who bore baggage of
suicidal attempts and crushed babies.

But, what were you about?

Smoke circles from hookah sessions
over Macbeth debates—
stories of pot and perico
while drinking Cosmos and Rolling Rocks—
dining table transports
through world-wide sustenance—

(Lady Macbeth was the mastermind, by the way.)

You came to me
with confusion in your heart
warped by the smell of jasmine from my hair.
You stayed
while I puked the end of an era,
in that haze of where I was
and
where I thought I would be.
You made love to me,
under crimson moons followed by
heart-shaped chocolates.

But I was still like,

Is this all a ploy?
I'm a broke bitch with a
caution sign on my pussy—
            and on my mind.

You saw the painted smile on my frown—
the moments of utter euphoria one second,
and the drop to an abysmal lava pool the next.

You reassured me,

we are both children,
walking on the least chosen path
of cactus stalks and beheaded roses,
dodging the angry dragons in
the dark clouds of our psyche.
We fight when the bikini-clad ring girl
does not hold round numbers around us
but hold mirrors up to us.

Look, none of this ain't really us, you know.
Maybe it really just the shit in us.

Our bed, wet and warmed by the presence of
our unity will feed whatever it is we do have,
What we have—not constrained by definition.

## Leading Up to

When we shared a medium fries from McD's
a couple of years into our puberty, we walked
through Crotona Park past the swimming pool,
crack vials, and cracked walkways. Tall trees
created our separated space. You tossed the
empty red McD's envelope and held my hand
with playful care. Your hands, so soft that I fell;
you led me to a scratched bench. We sat, smelling
the chlorine and hearing the children from the pool.

You had dreams.
I had fantasies.
You wanted to be a seed carried away;
I told you I was this bench.

We are young, you said. Maybe you thought you
would take this bench since I thought I would
pan fry the bird destined to carry you away. Then
it happened. Your lips tasted like biting into a ripe
Southern Bronx peach. My arms hugged your neck,
your mouth hugged my breath. The strings of our
pubertal energies danced between the branches
above us. How long did we kiss?

# Masturbation with THAT Magazine

*My Love Letter to Prince*


Taint her body with
    Regal water
        Engage in a kiss
            Because that kiss will slow this

Little Red Corvette down
    You know you are insatiable to her—
        Keep her body in your
            dirty little cage

Die for her?
    Call, beg
        Call her name
            Because she knows,

She can be nasty with you—
    She will touch it, so that it could explode.
        She will be, whatever you want her to be
            It will be, forever you.

You truly adore her with
    This spiritual sexuality journey
        Until the end of time—
            Are these tears from her or from the angels above?

You are filthy cute,
    A beautiful one.
        So come back to her, messiah
            Bring her flowers back to life.

Come back to her, you,
Always, the beautiful one.

## Dates

When he went
to Jackson Heights,
he brought back
parathas and masalas
for our children
and dates for me.
He is no longer
here, but the
container of dates
stay unopened
in my cupboard.

# You Asked How I Was Doing

I am wondering how to tell my body that it will
not have you again, how to tell my neck that it
will not feel your lips, how to convince my mind
it cannot dance with eager thoughts of you in me—
that in those quiet moments of solace, in my stillness,
I cannot message you, and ask,
When will I see you again? I wonder how I can
make my body understand that your hands
were pulled away from me, that your thoughts of
me are now forced into another spectrum of existence.

You asked how I was feeling,
I told you my feelings were meaningless.
But you have always been honest, you said.
Only when I am open, I said—

I am not sure how to walk from
being chosen, then unchosen.

# Do Things, Want

i want to do things to you that
i only do in the space between
my temples. with
my hand,
i feel your strength and make real
        the imaginations in
my daydreams
i submit within my desires but
        settle within
my                       reality.

# i just wanna...

i know i am supposed to play coy   and not admit   i would be needy   i would
appear insecure    i would be unrespectable    i know to want you means to
give you the reign and let you lead    i am supposed to pretend that I don't want
you   to kind of make myself noticed   but not really   but really   to pretend
i don't like you     but really   but not really    so that you can make that first
move    i know i am supposed to water your male ego with my hidden thoughts
of wrapping my legs around you

and sit    and      wait                          for                                                              you

be all the man you are     humble into my submission and conquer    the truth
of a man is in the girth of his compliance        my right hand touched your arm
once     i cum with my right hand

i just wanna...

now      i want you to come to me when you need church    be on your knees
while you eat your god   i want to   play bitches brew    while i gyrate on you to
the bass beats    your ego is not what i want between my legs    you are   glancing
at my direction and i wonder    am i just another person in the crowd    your lips
i want to bite    i imagine my lips on yours            your tongue  in  my  mouth
my breathing synchronizing with yours    your hands     pull me closer to you
right now    mom taught me to take what i want in life    cuz ain't nobody gonna
give it me    i want us to meet with no words    i don't need the next day flowers
or check-ins    all of what is your life and of what is my life       die in orgasmic
screams     should i mention   i am multi-orgasmic    i want you to levitate in
my submission    on my knees    making my head move towards where you want
it to go    my tongue   licking the line that divides your abs with brushes of my
teeth on your nipples    a kiss    again   i write this poem    perusing your page
knowing that my fantasy is my discretion                be discreet    you want
me       broken by your touch        don't need you to call me                unless
you want it                          again

# a god

his voice
at times
is not clear—
i hear him
but i don't know if it is
him
or myself.
i want to hear him—

## a devil

i see the light
the moment is
an ephemeral
abyss into a
world of no returns.
i hear the child
voices of wishes
and the paper
folding into
aerial devices.
the past of all
that is present
in my stream of
thoughts push
into the thoughts i
want for myself.

## Still Crucified

lack of desire
or the suppression of it
crucifies the innocent body.
we start in one place,
process through journeys
of men, but still end where
we started. we look up
through the clouds as
the sun shines on our
pained face. we don't feel
forsaken but redeemed
in the opium of existential
success. crucified, arms open
with blood dripping from the
holes of our palms and red
fading in our clothes, we feel
the pointing of approval
and the tears of despair—

## Mommy's Nails

I wish the doctor would not have
cut her nails. They were cut to
properly fit an oximeter.

She used to get her nails done every
Saturday morning, always the first
person at the nail salon.

She had her favorite nail technician,
and her favorite nail colors. They
were her nails, grown from her skin.
Not acrylic.

I wish the funeral director would
have used acrylic, for her to have
nails when she was in the coffin. I

would have painted them
rouge.

## Hosanna

He leans over the sink holding his cup of
chamomile tea. A Spanish Christian song
whose chorus is "Hosanna" plays in the
adjacent room. Lights are flashing above
him, as if he were in an interrogation room.
I wonder why he has not changed the bulb
yet. I, in the hallway, stand at the wall
dividing the Christianity and reality.
I put my money on the tea. I think the
tea will have more of a chance healing
the food poisoning than the music yelling
"Hosanna."

## (Jordan)

nothing else could have happened—
convinced i completed the tower others failed at building,
at the whim of failed loves that
sliced my core into safe detachments

did not know what would happen—
i was the degenerate composer
waiting to be possessed by the next note.
i faced you, then fear turned me around
just to face a dead end.
you stayed with still temerity
offering your prescription for my dormant intensity

what happened when i faced you—
when i faced you
and became drenched in your birthing qualities,
destruction of passions out of the lust I knew,
leaving remnants of regrets

so much is about to happen—
the fear that carried me into an abyss of
freedoms i thought i enjoyed in
baseless encounters became the ending.
i am young, still with passion but led by deity,
yielded by intellect

i just needed you to turn me
into me.

## Locs Up

He said he liked my hair up
he enjoyed the lines of my neck going into the curve between
my shoulders. I always keep it up now.

I am submissive, I once told him. He kissed the lines on my neck
then bit each wet kiss, leaving purple colored marks.
I liked the marks. They looked like birth marks before they
faded—

like his affection.

I liked the stinging feeling of his lips
the gripping feeling of his bite.

My scented oil of golden desert, you said,
tasted like slices of pineapple

I still keep my hair up. I flip my head down
to gather my hair with two strands of my locs.
I tie the two locs, putting my hair in a ponytail.
I wrap the hair around the tied part to make
a bun, then tuck in the loose loc strands.
I look into the reflection of the window to
check my bun.

If I see him,
I want him to see
that I still submit.

## The Poet

i want him to read my body
the way he reads a poem.
i want to wrap my legs around
him, using my hips to maneuver
him around so that i can orgasm
right when i am squeezing him
closer to my body, his face
close to mine. when i face
him, we both feel strong,
lifted. feeling young again.

## August [aw-GUHST]

August is such a pretty word, a word I included in our vocabulary list from the short story, "A Rose for Emily." I have never seen the word used in any other text I have read. (I figured, if I must teach dead white men to my black and brown students, then I will teach a story written by a man who held other dead white men accountable for being white men.) I mispronounced the word, at first, pronouncing it as the month, but a student suggested that maybe, because it is not the month, the pronunciation must be different. I Googled the pronunciation, and she was right. When used in its proper pronunciation, it represents the ethereal value of images a mind subconsciously connect, like schools of wizadry, visually powerful video games, or the cute girl or boy from Science class.

When entering this lesson of, what we call in secondary academia, five- and ten-dollar words (as if my students would get paid if they used those words, by an elusive bank who actually cares about the success of my South Bronx students), we discussed the value of increasing one's personal vocabulary. Unfamiliar words become familiar, they all agreed, and the variety of words would allow them to have strong arguments when conversing with others. One student, a Special Education student with an Individualized Educational Program, immediately welcomed the opportunity of learning vocabulary words because doing so, he said, would make him smarter.

I like the word "august," emphasis on the second syllable. My students know they will be *venerated* by an impressive vocabulary, and will be *highly respected* by all who hear them speak.

# Scar

It was hot combs with Dax
Boar brushes with blow dryers,
Deep conditioners and coconut oil
sitting under the dome dryer
extra-large rollers
Dax Grease and Pink Lotion
Vaseline and Queen Helene
It was all, to make the women in my family
Feel more comfortable with my hair.

I love you, mi mama me dijo,
and I am going to tell you—
If only you had my hair, or your sister's—
The world is not going to be good to you.
The world is not going to accept you—

Your hair, will never be good enough
Your hair, es pelo de negro
Y en este mundo, el negro es malo
Tu pelo, your hair, es malo
You, mijita, are not the bad one
Es tu pelo

Let's go for a walk, she said
As we always did on the Concourse
Conversations of 7th grade classroom gossip
A poem I just read
Sneakers I wanted

That day, was the day

the salon          on the Concourse          the salon owner   her daughter, in her
image          their hair, long          Farrah Fawcett layered   they promised
my mother     they would fix   my hair          tingle   cream smoothens out
my curls          stirs my ancestors          leaves my hair flat          hair  is  being
fixed     they say     my hair will look like my mother's          pale-skinned girls
will let me play with them          that cute light-skinded boy will see me


burn     one spot          then another spot          a tear     I hear     stop crying
this is good for you                    this will help you          a comb on the burning
spot     the skin, I feel from the inside     my hair  will look like my mother's just
this burn          this carrying of the heavy cross          to get to my new life
          life will be          like my new hair          good


fire     the house that is my scalp          the cute boy     the girls   my mother's
hair     my sister's hair   carry the cross          mi pelo malo     all          burned
down     Farrah Fawcett


          pelo de negro became plastic hair of white


scabs     I pick one          I scratched it off          I can remove the pain but I will
keep the hair          hair does not grow from there now          I    don't    get
pelo de negro   I don't get pelo de blanco          I have a scar     scar of when I
was being          fixed.

# Nose, African and Arawak

It is my mother and father.

My mother gave me the round that protrudes.
She also gave me the appearance of two straight lines,
if viewed from the front. At close view, the shape
takes on the thinness on top of that, that lends to the
immediate roundness.

My father gave me the thinness on top. My mother
used to say curse her nose and tell me that I should
have gotten my father's nose, fully.

I never liked its shape because of the
combination of the round and thin.

Now, I celebrate its shape, with two piercings:
a nostril ring from a piercing gun, done
at a kiosk in a mall in Ecuador, and a septum ring
from an East Village piercing shop.

I do have two pimple scars and freckles.

I look at the scars, wondering why I still
get pimples; yet, I know that if I actually
stop spiking my coffee with milk and
sleep normal hours, I would not be writing
about pimples right now.

I also know that my last name is Scottish,
and my freckles are probably of Scottish influence.

Or, because I have dark skin that is very sensitive,
the spots may not even be freckles but remnants
of hyperpigmentation.

## Lipstick, Eyeliner, Pause
*for Neil*

The façade was defined by a
man bleeding on a cross,
And that façade created a
space between
acceptance and detachment—
Where you will be cool,
if you were anything but you—
Where children, who had just
seen their sperm and blood,
Had a false faith in their
nascent familiarity with adulthood.
Where you were attached to those
Beliefs that felt right
At the time, but—

My god, really, ran on
red lipstick and charcoal eyeliner.

One day, though, I,
fatigued by the race of
running away from me,
You, inspired by
A guardian angel,
You said to me—

*Hey, you know, you*
*are beautiful the way are.*
*I mean, you are pretty,*
*regardless, but how you look,*
*just you—*

You saw my born face, and
reassured me that the created
face was an illusion solely appropriate
for this masquerade party called
Catholic high school.
You weren't that viejo sucio who sold
numbers on the corner, who always tried
speaking to me on some man-woman-level
shit. You were not that
19-year old, who lured me with
Pac-Man then conquered me with his penis.
You were not that kid riding on the
fallacious, so-called looseness
of a coquettish girl who smiled at all,
Since attention from home was none

You were—
Well, this other kid—
The mother's arms after birth—
Who felt the path my pain could have taken me.
I wanted to fall backwards, now knowing
That my future, in its new path,
Would catch me and float my adolescence
into iron womanhood.

Did you walk on water, my friend?

You *are* the angelito,
Telling me, all is well, little one
All is well when
you are just you.

**End**

I.
my fear
carries me.

II.
thank you for saving my
tears.

III.
you make my
reality
seem
inadequate

IV.
you are a cloud
in the shape of
a dinosaur

# Dear Brother

I understand the need to look for a space away from
reality. I have also found myself sleeping in anonymous
spaces to ward off inebriation and welcome the shadows
of my fears. I have sat on the edge of the Grand Canyon
and have wondered how long my body would stay in air
before it hits ground. Should I turn my body, to face up,
so that my face remains pleasant to the eye of all who will
look down on me when in my final box? Face up or face
down—like my life—would probably not make a difference.
The drink, I would rather have injected into my veins, because
I hear injection would give me death while still breathing.
I can be happy and blend into crowds and be funny and be
liked and be a self that is not my self but a mimed part of
myself.  Or, maybe the id part of myself released by the
ethanol, lifting the veil of all I want to be and all I hate of myself.

## DIY: How to Commit a Murder-Suicide While Daughter is in the Apartment

Step 1: Call ex-wife. Invite ex-wife over.
Tell her you have money to give her,
because you have not given her money
in a while. Tell her to bring daughter
because you want to tell daughter that you
love her, twice, maybe three times.

Step 2: Convince ex-wife that the visit
is simply to give her the child support
you have not given in a while. That
you have been working, getting help,
changing your life. That you miss your
daughter. That you are aware of the order
of protection against you, but not seeing
your daughter is torturous. Beg ex-wife.
Appeal to her sensitive side. Tell her that
what they are going through should not
interfere with relationship with
daughter.

Step 3: Load gun. Two bullets

Step 4: Let ex-wife in. Let daughter in.
Hug your daughter. Tell your daughter
you love her. Walk her to the living room.
Turn the television on. Tell daughter you
love her. Put the volume on high. Add
more volume. Yell to daughter, over the
loud television, Daddy will always love you.

<u>Step 5</u>: Close the living room door. Take a nail, and hammer nail down against living room door. Nail door shut.

<u>Step 6</u>:

<u>Step 7</u>: Close toilet seat. Sit down.
One bullet left.

<u>Step 8</u>:

# Rollerskating with Jesus on the Grand Concourse

I rollerskate on the Concourse
past art deco buildings and bodegas
I use the strength of my legs to push me forward
the bend of my knees for momentum
the gaze towards the courthouse to keep my balance

Yet, I fall.
(No, I did not wear any protective gear.
I just rolled with my faith in myself.)

My knee, its skin scraped off
blood dripping.
The scrape must have covered my whole knee.

My brother tells me good, you are learning.
He kneels down and looks at the scrape.
he walks me to an open hydrant and takes a
handkerchief from his back pocket to clean the scrape.
(Yes, we used water from an open hydrant,
No, I am not sure where that handkerchief was
and no, we did not use Neosporin.)

He tells me to sit on the edge of the sidewalk,
next to his Sony boombox.
He increases the volume.
*Gimme me a "ho"*
*if you got your funky bus fare*
*ho—ho—ho*

His afro looks like a Jesus halo
The wheels grow from his feet, he
moonwalks then spins, first on both feet
then on one leg, makes undulations with
unseen lines.
He spins and spins
*bip bomp bam, alakazam,*
like a record
after a strong scratch release,
crossing his legs with his
body tilted on one side
then switching direction
with his body tilted the other side

then he falls.
(Yes, my brother fell. Even the best of them have to fall, right?)
A pebble that made him fall.
He smiles at himself, looks at me
with the same smile, and tells me
we all have to fall sometime
but we learn when we get back up
He held his hand out for me to get up.
I took his hand and we skated
my Jesus and me on the Concourse
towards the courthouse.

# My Brother's Keeper

My brother was, again, drunk, lying on the top step of the big church on the hill, the one with the bright bronze doors. He was yelling, fuck you, to the doors of the church. He lifted his head just to say, fuck you, then put his head back down on the step, closed his eyes, and cradled an empty bottle of Bacardi the way he cradled his stuffed elephant toy when he was a child. Our neighbor told my mother over the phone, your son is drunk again. Find your drunk son on the steps of that big church on the hill. The neighbor said that no one walked towards him to shush him, a parishioner did not come out to walk him in, the priest did not stop watching child porn in his private quarters to offer forgiveness, and Jesus did not step down from his cross to make my brother a disciple, or even share a bottle of wine with him. That's why he said, fuck you, to the big bronze doors of the church, the neighbor said. Jesus turned water into wine for people who could have had a wedding without wine, but my brother needed that wine to get drunk to keep living. This ain't no wedding; this is life.

My mother, begged my father for a ride. Fuck no, he said. Fuck that drunk. You see, my brother was not my father's son. My father washed his hands of any responsibility for him. My father did not have any guilt, of what he could have done wrong with my brother, if a wrong decision in his childhood made my brother so broken that he had to say, fuck you, to the bright bronze doors of the big church on the hill, then fall asleep cradling the empty bottle of Bacardi, the way he cradled his stuff elephant when he was a child. My mother, she lived with some guilt, I am sure, so she begged my father. Please, take me to him. I need help carrying him to his bed. Please, drive me to him. Fuck that, my father said. I may lose my parking spot. I need to wake up early in the morning. What would that teach him, if his mother constantly runs to his aid whenever he falls drunk on the top step of the big church on the hill, the one with the bright bronze doors. My father still drove her, though. My father really was saying, fuck you, to the man who never responded to my brother's letters. That man sent that stuffed elephant to my brother with a promise of connection, then cut that connection as soon as my brother said, I love you, Pop. I love you. Thank you for the elephant. I love you.

He was on the top step of the church, cradling an empty bottle of Bacardi. The bright bronze doors shined behind my brother, and my mother, step by step by step by step by step, walked up to the doors of the church to get to my brother. In that bible story, the son returns to the family, but at this church, the mother was returning to the son. My mother, went to him and pulled the bottle away from his arms. Startled, he yelled, fuck you, when the bottle was out of his arms, and my mother said, This is your mother. Watch your mouth. Get up now. Someone may see you. He said, fuck you, again. My mother said, we don't want people talking about you being a drunk outside of a church. Come. Stand up. He said fuck you again, then cried. My mother said, don't cry out here, son. Let's go to your bed. She carried the stuffed elephant, I mean, the empty bottle, I mean the stuffed elephant, I mean the empty bottle, because leaving the empty bottle at the church would be disrespectable to Jesus and crosses and saints and solid bronze doors and priests who watch child porn. She placed his arm around her shoulder, placed her arm around his waist, and with the empty bottle of Bacardi, stuffed elephant, empty bottle of Bacardi, walked to the car. The car running, my father looked ahead, waiting patiently to hear the backseat car door close. This was her burden, she knew. But she loved him. If she was the only person who did love him, she was going to love him.

## ACKNOWLEDGEMENTS

"La Gringa First Ride to Lost Hondos"
originally published in BOMB magazine (Winter 2023 issue)

"Mango," "Mind Fuck,""i just wanna,'
originally published in the chapbook,
*Mango*
Ocean Taste Publications

"Masturbation With THAT Magazine"
originally published in
*I Only Wanted One Time To See You Laughing: Prince Tribute Anthology:*
*Prince Tribute Anthology*
Yellow Chair Review

"Peacock" and "Jordan"
workshopped with *Callaloo*, Oxford University, Summer, 2016

"Dear Brother"
originally published in
*Escape Wheel* by Mad Gleam Press

"Bronx Wild Turkey Off the Bruckner"
originally published in *Naked in the City*
NeuroNautic Press

# ABOUT THE AUTHOR

Mercy Tullis-Bukhari is a poet, essayist, and fiction writer who focuses on the woman experience through individuality, motherhood, and sexuality. She published two books of poetry titled *Smoke* (Blind Beggar Press, Inc.) and *Mango* (Ocean Taste Publications). She is a Callaloo Fellow, an MFA recipient in Creative Writing from The College of New Rochelle, and the Poet Laureate of the New York University 30th Anniversary Celebration Gala. Mercy was named one of the "8 Authors Bringing Afro-Latina Stories to the Forefront" by *Remezcla* magazine and was a Pushcart Prize nominee in 2016 for her essay, "Black Dolls for Everyone." Mercy teaches high school English Language Arts in the Southeast section of The Bronx and is completing her first novel. She currently lives in New Rochelle, NY, with her two children.

*Mercy would like to thank Brian Sheffield
for his guidance and support editing
different versions of this manuscript.*